# Scary Creatures
## of the
# WETLANDS

Written by
Penny Clarke

Franklin Watts®
An Imprint of Scholastic Inc.
NEW YORK • TORONTO • LONDON • AUCKLAND • SYDNEY
MEXICO CITY • NEW DELHI • HONG KONG
DANBURY, CONNECTICUT

Created and designed
by David Salariya

**Author:**

**Penny Clarke** is an author and editor who specializes in nonfiction books for children. She has written books on natural history, rain forests and volcanoes, as well as books on different periods of history. She used to live in central London, but thanks to modern technology, she has now fulfilled her dream of being able to live and work in the countryside.

**Artists:**

John Francis
Mark Bergin
Carolyn Scrace
Li Sidong
Julian Baker

**Series Creator:**

**David Salariya** was born in Dundee, Scotland. He established The Salariya Book Company in 1989. He has illustrated a wide range of books and has created many new series for publishers in the UK and overseas. He lives in Brighton with his wife, illustrator Shirley Willis, and their son.

**Editors:** Tanya Kant, Stephen Haynes

**Editorial Assistant:** Rob Walker

**Picture Research:**
Mark Bergin, Carolyn Franklin

PAPER FROM
SUSTAINABLE
**FORESTS**

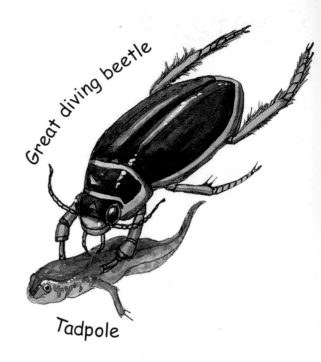

Great diving beetle

Tadpole

© The Salariya Book Company Ltd MMVIII
All rights reserved. No part of this book may be reproduced, stored in a retrieval system or transmitted in any form or by any means, electronic, mechanical, photocopying, recording or otherwise, without the written permission of the copyright owner.

Created, designed, and produced by
**The Salariya Book Company Ltd**
25 Marlborough Place, Brighton BN1 1UB

A CIP catalog record for this title is available from the Library of Congress.

ISBN-13: 978-0-531-21749-8 (Lib. Bdg.)
978-0-531-21903-4 (Pbk.)
ISBN-10: 0-531-21749-3 (Lib. Bdg.)
0-531-21903-8 (Pbk.)

Published in the United States by Franklin Watts
An Imprint of Scholastic Inc.
557 Broadway
New York, NY 10012

Printed in China

# Contents

Painted turtle

Swordtail

Electric eel

# What Is a Wetland?

A wetland is just that: land that is swampy and wet all or part of the time. Oceans, seas, rivers, and big lakes are not wetlands. Wetlands occur all over the world, in both warm and cold regions. In this book you'll meet a few of the creatures and plants that live in wetlands— and some of them are really scary!

Everything shown here lives in a wetland, though not all in the same one! The animals are not all drawn to the same scale.

African pygmy goose

Nile crocodile

Blister beetle

Water lilies

Hippopotamus

Jeweled cichlid

Wetlands can be made up of fresh, **brackish**, or salty water. Most living things have evolved to live in only one kind of wetland.

African fish eagle

Sitatunga

Yellow bittern

African jacana

Malachite kingfisher

Otters

Purple heron

Dragonfly

Dwarf mouth-brooder

Pirate butterfly

Emerald tree frog

Tigerfish

African pike

# Where Are the Wetlands?

There are wetlands on every continent except Antarctica. Rivers are not wetlands, but wetlands often form beside rivers. Each year, for example, the Nile and Amazon rivers flood huge areas along their banks, forming wetlands. Until these areas dry up, they are home to huge numbers of insects, birds, **amphibians**, and creatures that prey on them.

The alligator snapping turtle lives in the Florida Everglades. It has a pink, wormlike "lure" in its mouth. When the turtle lies still in the water with its mouth wide open, fish are easy **prey**.

Frogs, toads, and newts are amphibians. They start their lives i the water as **larvae**, breathing through gills, but change into adul that live on land and have lungs.

North America

Everglades

Tropic of Cancer

Central America

Equator

Amazon basin

Tropic of Capricorn

South America

Major wetland areas

Alligator snapping turtle

Mangroves

Mangrove trees form swamps around coasts in **tropical** regions. Their tangled **aerial roots** trap **silt** and vegetation.

## Marbled newt

## Willow tree

Newts live in **temperate** wetlands all over the world.

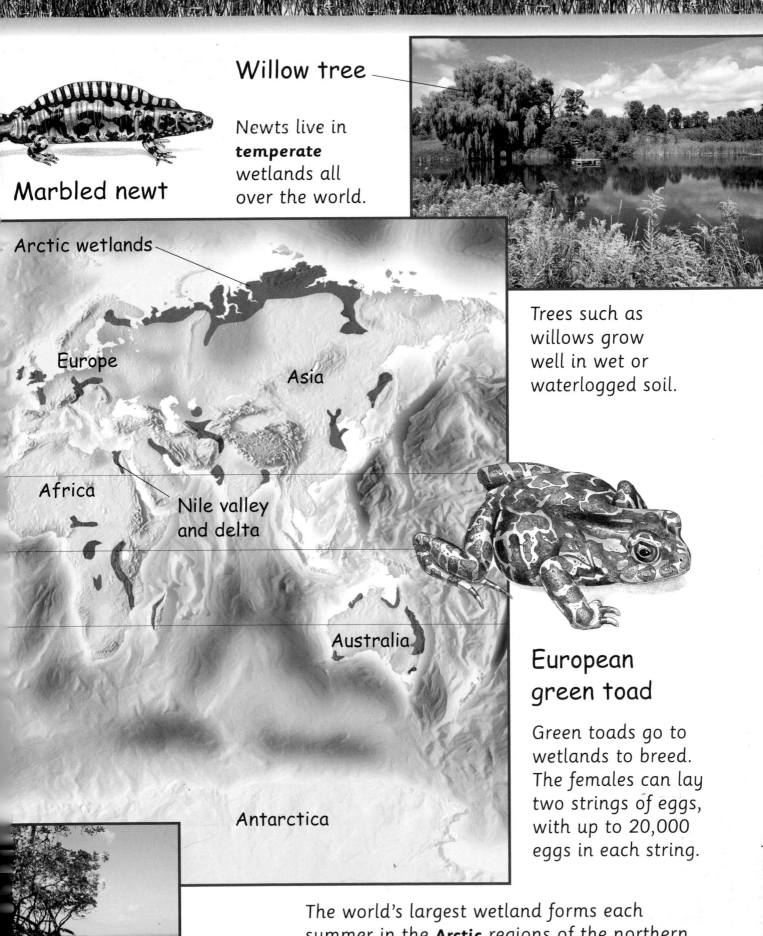

Arctic wetlands

Europe

Asia

Africa

Nile valley and delta

Australia

Antarctica

Trees such as willows grow well in wet or waterlogged soil.

## European green toad

Green toads go to wetlands to breed. The females can lay two strings of eggs, with up to 20,000 eggs in each string.

The world's largest wetland forms each summer in the **Arctic** regions of the northern **hemisphere**. As the long winter ends, the frozen ground thaws to form a huge swamp.

# What Plants Grow in Wet Places?

Most plants rot in wet soil, but some have evolved so they don't. Reeds grow through shallow water, water lilies float on the surface, and a few plants, like the Canadian pondweed, grow underwater. To grow, plants must absorb water and **nutrients** through their roots. Swampy soil has few nutrients, so some plants, like the pitcher plant, have found surprising ways to survive.

Most of these plants and animals live in the damp areas at the edges of ponds, lakes, and streams. Big pike lurk in the shadow of the reeds, waiting for their prey.

Water lily

Frogs

Pike

## Did You Know?

The world's largest water lily grows in the **sluggish** backwaters of the Amazon River. The leaves of the roya water lily (*Victoria amazonica*) can be more than 6.5 feet (2 m) across.

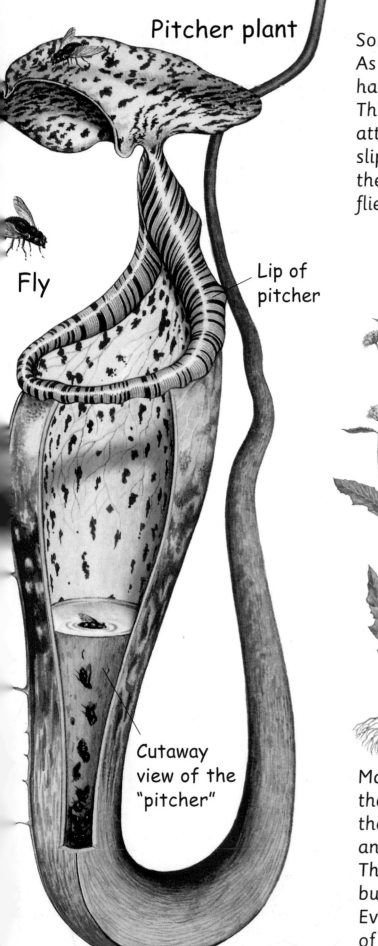

**Pitcher plant**

Fly

Lip of
pitcher

Cutaway
view of the
"pitcher"

Some plants survive by eating insects!
As its name suggests, the pitcher plant
has a deep pouch like a pitcher or jar.
This contains liquid chemicals that
attract flies. The flies land on the
slippery lip of the pitcher and fall into
the liquid. The plant then digests the
flies and absorbs the nutrients it needs.

Yellow
cress

Water
crowfoot

Butterbur

Many wetland plants don't rot because
they grow in places that are not wet all
the time. Plants like butterbur, cress,
and crowfoot grow in cooler climates.
They grow best when the ground is wet,
but can survive when it is only damp.
Even when wetlands dry out, the seeds
of some plants still survive.

9

# Does Africa Have Wetlands?

Africa has **seasonal** wetlands that form in the rainy season and dry up in the summer heat. These wetlands are vital for Africa's wildlife. The Nile, the world's longest river, flows 4,160 miles (6,695 km) from central Africa north to the Mediterranean Sea. Vast areas of wetland exist on the Nile's banks, as well as on the banks of the Congo River in central Africa.

**X-Ray Vision**

Hold the next page up to the light to see the hippo's skull.

*See what's inside*

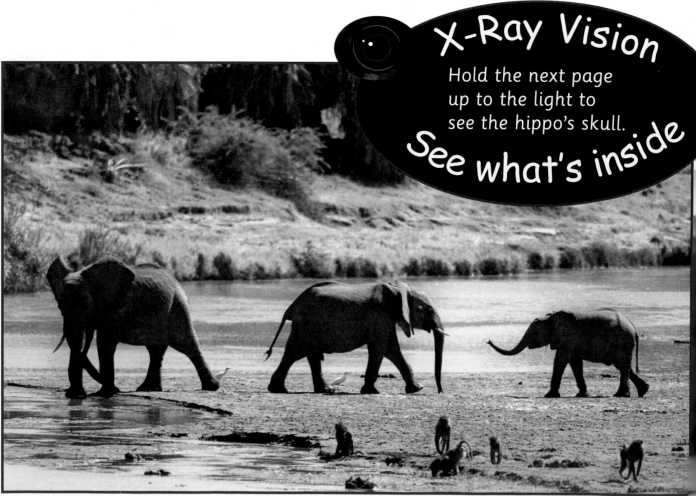

Elephants and baboons by a river that is shrinking in Africa's summer heat

Hippos live in African wetlands. They spend much of their time in the shallow rivers, lakes, or swamps next to grasslands. They are **herbivores**—they eat plants—but that doesn't mean they are friendly!

Turn the page to learn more about these scary creatures.

"Hippo" is short for "hippopotamus," which means "river horse" in Greek.

Eye socket

Upper canine teeth

Tusks (lower canine teeth)

Powerful jawbone

The hippo's "tusks" are really very large **canine teeth**.

# Are Hippos Dangerous?

Yes, even though they are herbivores! Hippos live in groups, and the males fight to be leader of their group and to claim territory on the riverbank. They will also attack people in the water, and even small boats. Hippos may look clumsy, but they swim and dive well, helped by the four webbed toes on each foot.

## Did You Know?

When hippos swim underwater, they close their nostrils to keep the water out.

Hippos eat so much vegetation that they keep wetland edges clear of plants. This allows other animals to get to the water.

Fights between male hippos often cause serious injuries, but rarely death.

# What Is a Delta?

Big rivers carry huge quantities of fine soil, called silt. As the river approaches the sea, the water flows more slowly and the silt sinks to the bottom. Over thousands of years, this silt builds up to form an area of low-lying land called a **delta**. Deltas are *fertile* places, so there is plenty of food and water. They can be good places for humans and wildlife to live, but there is always a danger of floods.

This delta land lies only a little higher than the river, so flooding is a constant danger—and **global warming** could make the danger even worse.

# Wetland predator

**Black-necked stork**

The black-necked stork lives in the wetlands of Asia and Australia. Its long legs help it to wade through the water as it creeps toward its prey. With its long neck and beak, it quickly stabs the water, catching its prey by surprise.

When a river flows through low-lying land, it often forms wide curves known as meanders. When the river floods, it may break its banks and flow straight across. Then the meanders are cut off to form U-shaped "oxbow" lakes.

**Meanders**

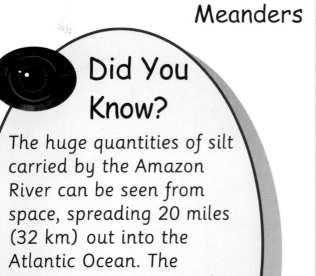

## Did You Know?

The huge quantities of silt carried by the Amazon River can be seen from space, spreading 20 miles (32 km) out into the Atlantic Ocean. The Amazon carries so much fresh water that it dilutes the ocean's saltiness for 200 miles (320 km) from its mouth.

**Bromeliad**

Wetlands aren't always on the ground! In rain-forest trees, pools of water create miniature wetlands where tiny frogs and insects live and breed.

# Are All Wetlands Big?

No, but creatures live even in small ones! Most frogs and toads lay their eggs at the edges of wetlands. The eggs hatch into tadpoles—hunters of tiny insects and fish larvae. But other hunters lie in wait for the tadpoles.

The dragonfly nymph is a dragonfly at an early stage in its life. It lurks in shallow water, grabbing tadpoles in its strong jaws. Diving beetles also feed on tadpoles. That's why frogs and toads have to lay so many eggs.

**Crane fly**

**Dragonfly nymph**

**Tadpoles**

Pied
flycatcher

May bug

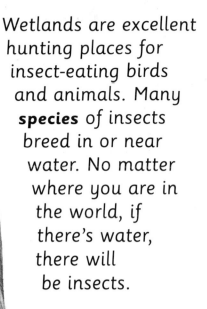

Wetlands are excellent
hunting places for
insect-eating birds
and animals. Many
**species** of insects
breed in or near
water. No matter
where you are in
the world, if
there's water,
there will
be insects.

Grey wagtail

Pond skater

Dragonfly larvae

Caddis fly

Great
diving
beetle

Stickleback

17

# What's the Biggest Wetland?

The world's largest wetland is also one of the world's coldest regions: the **tundra** of northern Europe and Asia. During the long Arctic winter the land is frozen hard. But in summer the top few inches of land thaw. The water cannot drain away because the ground below remains frozen, so the tundra becomes a huge bog. Insects breed in the millions, and then birds arrive to feed on them and breed. In turn, the large number of birds attracts many other **predators**.

A lone polar bear on the frozen winter tundra

Most birds fly south as the Arctic winter sets in, but some birds and mammals stay. The ptarmigan and Arctic fox lose their summer colors and turn white. This helps them survive in the snow-covered land. It provides **camouflage** for both hunter (the Arctic fox) and hunted (the ptarmigan).

## Arctic fox in summer

## Male ptarmigan changing to winter colors

Polar bears (opposite page) are among the world's scariest creatures, but they live in the Arctic where there are few people. These dangerous bears can outrun humans, and stand almost 10 feet (3 m) tall when they rear up on their hind legs.

### Did You Know?

"Reindeer" and "caribou" are different names for the same animal. The caribou of North America is the reindeer of northern Europe. Both males and females have antlers. Female reindeer are the only female deer in the world that have antlers.

## Reindeer/caribou

## X-Ray Vision

Hold the next page up to the light to see what's happening beneath the suface.

## See what's inside

## Giant armadillo

The thick vegetation on the Amazon's banks provides **habitats** for many creatures, from huge snakes to tiny insects.

Alligator

## Anaconda

Snakes are among the forest's scariest hunters. Their jaws expand so they can swallow prey much bigger than their heads.

Hoatzin

# Is the Amazon Rain Forest a Wetland?

Yes. Each year, from January to August, the Amazon River rises up to 30 feet (9 m) and floods vast areas of forest along its banks. Without the fertile silt the flood leaves behind, the forest could not grow. And without lush vegetation there would be none of this colorful wildlife.

Green-winged
macaws

Hyacinth macaw

Caiman

Capybara

Anaconda

Collared peccary

Electric eel

Catfish

Caiman

Piranhas

Capybara

# What's Below the Surface?

Tapir

This pool in the Amazon rain forest is teeming with predators and prey. Capybaras are related to guinea pigs. They can grow to 4 feet (1.2 m) and are excellent swimmers, but that doesn't help when there's a hungry alligator or caiman nearby. Attracted by the smell of blood, piranhas quickly appear. On the bank an anaconda tackles a peccary (a wild pig). It coils its muscular body around the pig, and then it contracts its muscles, crushing the prey to death.

Brazilian tapirs live in swampy forests, sleeping by day and eating plants at night. Although they can grow up to 7 feet (2 m) long, they are hunted by anacondas and boas—snakes that kill by crushing their prey. After a tapir meal, the snake doesn't need to eat for months!

# What Other Scary Creatures Live in Wetlands?

One of the smallest and deadliest wetland creatures is the mosquito. Mosquitoes carry diseases that can kill humans, such as malaria, yellow fever, and dengue fever. For thousands of years, no one understood the link between mosquitoes and these diseases—but people knew that wetlands could be unhealthy places.

Did You Know?

In the 1880s, thousands of men building the Panama Canal died of malaria.

Piranhas

Catfish

Rosy tetra

Discus fish

Catfish use their "whiskers" to search for food in muddy water.

Electric eels really do electrocute their prey. They have special organs that can produce up to 500 volts of electricity. This isn't likely to kill a healthy human, but you'd get a very painful shock.

Electric organs

Electric eel

# Burmese python

Burmese pythons now live in Florida's Everglades. Originally imported as pets, they escaped or were let loose by their owners. They have made themselves at home and are now a threat to people and pets.

The estuarine crocodile of Southeast Asia and Australia can be up to 20 feet (6 m) long. It kills its prey—sometimes including humans—by dragging it underwater.

# Estuarine crocodile

# Do People Live in Wetlands?

Perhaps the best-known people living in wetlands today are the Madan or Marsh Arabs of southern Iraq. They live in the area of the Tigris and Euphrates rivers. The vast marshes between these two great rivers were drained and burned by the Iraqi government in the 1990s, but now the marshes are being restored.

It will take time for the marshes in southern Iraq to recover, but already the people have started to return—and so have birds and fish.

# Building in reed

The tall columns at the front of this Marsh Arab house are made from bundles of reeds.

The traditional *mudhif*, or village meeting house, of the Marsh Arabs is made entirely of reeds. Even the foundations are made of reeds packed down hard and covered with mud from the marshes. No other building materials are available in this area.

Inside an Iraqi mudhif

# Are Wetlands in Danger?

Sadly, many wetlands are in danger. As the world's population increases, wetlands are drained to create more land for homes. This destroys the habitats of many plants and animals. Drained land shrinks, and if it is below sea level, it will flood. If the land is flooded with salt water, it may be years before crops can grow there again.

Wetlands are often drained to make space for power stations or garbage dumps. The damage caused by pollution like this will last long into the future. Perhaps human beings are the scariest creatures of all!

## Tourists in Florida

Tourism can damage wetlands, but it can also help people to realize how beautiful and important they are. In the Florida Everglades, slow-moving boats take visitors through the waterways where they can see animals such as alligators (below) without harming them.

## Did You Know?

Wetlands around the Mediterranean Sea are essential stopovers for birds migrating between Europe and Africa.

# Wetland facts

Many wetland areas are covered with water plants. Birds called jacanas (see page 5) have very long toes that allow them to walk on the plants as they hunt insects, seeds, and snails.

There are some reports of estuarine crocodiles hunting humans in the swamps of northern Australia. Climbing a tree is not the answer—the crocs will lie in wait nearby.

In mangrove swamps from east Africa to Australia, fish called mudskippers live up to their name. They move quickly over muddy ground and climb mangrove roots to bask in the sun.

The ancient Egyptians owed their prosperity to the River Nile. The Nile floods each year. The silt left on the land by the flood makes it very fertile, so crops grow well there.

Small seasonal wetlands, especially in hot African climates, are in great danger if the annual rains don't occur. As the land dries up, the vegetation dies. If the **drought** lasts several years, the trees may never regrow.

In temperate regions, if the climate becomes drier, a wetland may become a woodland. First coarse grass moves in, then small shrubs. Larger shrubs follow, then trees take over.

The South African rain frog and bullfrog live in seasonal wetlands. They spend the dry periods underground and come to the surface only when it rains. Then they breed and feed. As the land dries out, they burrow deep into the ground again.

The huge leaves of the Amazon's royal water lily have air-filled ribs that help them float.

Crocodiles and alligators can replace their worn teeth. They grow new, sharp teeth that push the old ones out.

Much of the land in Bangladesh is below sea level. This sometimes causes disastrous floods.

Royal water lily

# Glossary

**aerial roots** Roots that are partly above ground.

**amphibian** A **cold-blooded** animal that can live on land or in water, but breeds only in water.

**Arctic** The part of the Earth north of the Arctic Circle.

**brackish** Slightly salty (referring to water).

**bromeliad** A type of plant that has fleshy leaves and often lives on other plants.

**camouflage** Markings or coloring on a creature that help it blend in with its surroundings.

**canine tooth** A pointed tooth used for tearing food.

**cold-blooded** Having a body temperature that changes with the temperature of the air.

**delta** A triangular area of land formed from silt deposited at a river's mouth.

**drought** A lack of rainfall.

**Equator** The imaginary line around the center of the Earth.

**fertile** Rich in nutrients.

**global warming** A gradual rise in the temperature of the Earth's atmosphere, partly caused by carbon dioxide and other polluting emissions.

**habitat** The place where a plant or animal lives naturally.

**hemispheres** The two halves of the Earth, north and south of the Equator.

**herbivore** An animal that eats only plants.

**larva** (plural **larvae**) A young animal that will change into a different form when it becomes an adult.

**nutrient** Anything that gives nourishment.

**predator** An animal that kills other animals for food.

**prey** An animal that is killed by another animal for food.

**seasonal** Changing with the seasons.

**silt** Very fine soil carried by rivers.

**sluggish** Slow-moving.

**species** A group of plants or animals that look alike, live in the same way, and produce young that do the same.

**temperate** Neither very hot nor very cold.

**tropical** Belonging to the tropics—the part of the Earth that lies between the Tropics of Cancer and Capricorn (see pages 6–7). This area has the warmest climate on Earth.

**tundra** The Arctic region where the soil below the surface never thaws.

# Index